Great
Rivers
of the World

THE GANGES

David Cumming

WORLD ALMANAC® LIBRARY

Please visit our web site at: www.worldalmanaclibrary.com
For a free color catalog describing World Almanac® Library's list of high-quality books and multimedia programs, call 1-800-848-2928 (USA) or 1-800-387-3178 (Canada). World Almanac® Library's fax: (414) 332-3567.

Library of Congress Cataloging-in-Publication Data

Cumming, David.
    The Ganges / David Cumming.
        p. cm. — (Great rivers of the world)
    Includes bibliographical references and index.
    Contents: The course of the river — The Ganges in history — Cities along the river — Farming, trade, and industry — Animals and plants — Environmental issues — Bathing and praying — The future.
    ISBN 0-8368-5443-8 (lib. bdg.)
    ISBN 0-8368-5450-0 (softcover)
    1. Ganges River (India and Bangladesh)—Juvenile literature. [1. Ganges River (India and Bangladesh).] I. Title. II. Series.
    DS485.G25C85   2003
    954'.1—dc21   2002033119

First published in 2003 by
World Almanac® Library
330 West Olive Street, Suite 100
Milwaukee, WI 53212 USA

Developed by Monkey Puzzle Media
Editor: Jane Bingham
Designer: Tim Mayer
Picture researcher: Lynda Lines
World Almanac® Library editor: Jim Mezzanotte
World Almanac® Library art direction: Tammy Gruenewald

Picture acknowledgements
Bruce Coleman Collection, 32 (Gerald S. Cubitt); Corbis, 4 (Chris Hellier); David Cumming, 1, 7, 9, 11, 16–17, 18, 22, 26, 36, 37, 42; Eye Ubiquitous, front cover (David Cumming), 20 (David Cumming), 43 (David Cumming); FLPA, 30 (Terry Whittaker), 33 (T. Stephenson/Earthviews); Robert Harding Picture Library, 5 (J.H.C. Wilson), 12 (Doug Traverso), 15 (British Museum, London), 24 (Duncan Maxwell), 25 (J.H.C. Wilson); Still Pictures, 21 (Mark Edwards), 23 (John Paul Kay), 28 (Shehzad Noorani), 31 (Don Hinrichson), 34 (Shehzad Noorani), 35 (Gunter Ziesler), 38 (Gil Moti), 40 (Shehzad Noorani), 41 (Shehzad Noorani), 45 (Don Hinrichson); Topham Picturepoint, 8, 13, 17 top (A.P.). Map artwork by Peter Bull.

Printed in the United States of America

1 2 3 4 5 6 7 8 9 07 06 05 04 03

CONTENTS

Introduction   4

1 The Course of the Ganges   6

2 The Ganges in History   12

3 Cities along the Ganges   18

4 Farming, Trade, and Industry   24

5 Animals and Plants   30

6 Environmental Issues   36

7 Bathing and Praying   42

8 The Future   44

Glossary   46

Time Line   47

Further Information   47

Index   48

INTRODUCTION

INTRODUCTION

A Long Journey

The waters of the Ganges River begin their journey high in the Himalaya Mountains in India. After a rapid descent, these waters snake slowly across the plains of northern India and into Bangladesh. Then they flow through the world's largest river **delta** into the Bay of Bengal.

The Ganges has many rivers, called **tributaries**, running into it. The Ganges and its tributaries drain water from an area that is a quarter of the size of India. This vast **basin** is one of the world's most crowded places. About 350 million people — more than one-twentieth of the world's population — live in the region. The soil in much of the basin is extremely fertile, so the region is an excellent one for farming. It provides millions of people with food.

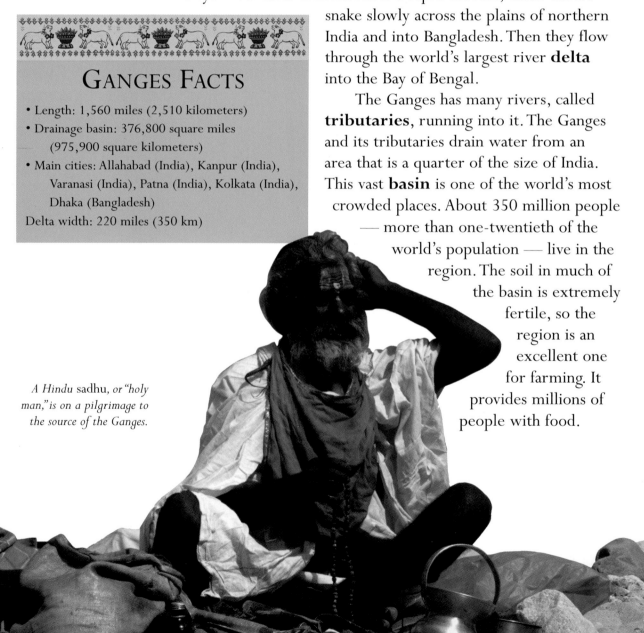

GANGES FACTS

- Length: 1,560 miles (2,510 kilometers)
- Drainage basin: 376,800 square miles (975,900 square kilometers)
- Main cities: Allahabad (India), Kanpur (India), Varanasi (India), Patna (India), Kolkata (India), Dhaka (Bangladesh)

Delta width: 220 miles (350 km)

A Hindu sadhu, *or "holy man," is on a pilgrimage to the source of the Ganges.*

The Ganges and India

The Ganges River has played a central role in the history of India. India's first settlements were built near the Ganges River, and fierce battles were fought against invading armies on its banks. In the twentieth century, Indians in the Ganges basin joined together to force the British to abandon control of India. The region is also the birthplace of two major religions, Hinduism and Buddhism.

The Indian city of Varanasi lies about halfway along the Ganges River's route to the sea.

For Hindus everywhere, the Ganges River is a holy river. They believe the river is the goddess Ganga, who has come down from Heaven to live on Earth. The river gets its name from this goddess.

A River of Problems?

The Ganges River is often in the news because of its pollution and the floods that it causes. The river remains heavily polluted, but the Indian government has taken some steps to clean it. The prevention of floods, however, is a harder problem to solve. India, Bangladesh, Nepal, and China will all have to work together to prevent flooding. Until these countries can agree on what needs to be done, the floods will only get worse.

Chapter 1

THE COURSE OF THE GANGES

THE COURSE OF THE GANGES

An Icy Source

High in the Himalaya Mountains of northwest India lies the Gangotri **glacier**. This colossal ice sheet is the **source** of the Ganges River. In winter, only a trickle of water drips from the ice. In May, however, the Sun melts the ice, producing an ice cave at the foot of the glacier. By June, a torrent of chilly water pours out of the cave. The entrance to the cave is called *Gaumukh*, which means "cow's mouth" in Hindi, the official language of India.

This map shows the course of the Ganges River and the main tributaries that flow into it.

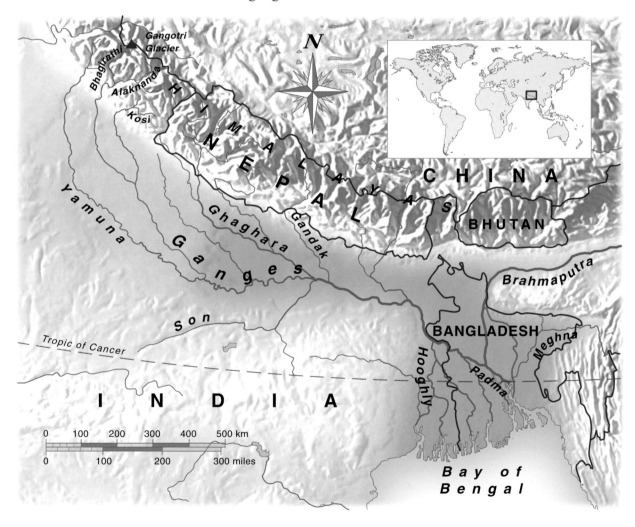

Although the source of the Ganges River is located at *Gaumukh*, the river that begins there is known as the Bhagirathi River. The fast-moving waters of the Bhagirathi make a steep descent. Near the village of Gangotri, only 10 miles (16 km) from *Gaumukh*, the river is already a staggering 2,950 feet (900 meters) lower than it is at its source.

GANGOTRI GLACIER

Altitude: 12,795 feet (3,900 m)

Length: 15 miles (24 km)

Width: 5 miles (8 km)

The Upper Ganges

The steep descent of the Bhagirathi River makes it powerful. Helped by the grinding action of rocks and stones swept along by the current, the river has **eroded** a narrow, steep-sided **gorge** in the rock. The gorge snakes down to the village of Devprayag, where the Bhagirathi meets the Alaknanda River. From this point onward, the combined waters of the two rivers are known as the Ganges River.

The Ganges River begins here, at the village of Devprayag. The Bhagirathi River is on the left and the Alaknanda is on the right.

The Middle Ganges

At the town of Hardwar, the waters of the Ganges River leave the mountains and begin traveling across the flat land of northern India. This region is known as the Ganges plain. Without a steep slope, the river's waters move more slowly, and the river no longer has the energy to dig a deep gorge in the earth. It wanders slowly across the plain, and its valley becomes wider and shallower.

This bridge, called Lakshman Jhula, crosses the Ganges just north of Hardwar, where the river is still very narrow.

Narrow and Wide

Beyond Hardwar, the Ganges almost vanishes, due to the Upper Ganges Canal (see page 24). Since opening in 1854, the canal has robbed the river of much of its water.

At this stage, the Ganges shrinks to a large stream. It does not become a river again until the town of Allahabad, where it is joined by the Yamuna River. This river is the first important tributary of the Ganges and provides it with a large amount of water. The Ganges does not become a major river again, however, until the town of Patna. At this stage, three more large tributaries — the Ghaghara, Son, and Gandak Rivers — feed into it.

The Ghaghara River is the largest tributary of the Ganges River in India. This river pours 20,766 million gallons (78,579 million liters) of water into the Ganges every year.

Beyond the town of Patna, the Ganges River becomes extremely wide. This photograph shows local fishermen in their boats.

Beyond Patna, the Ganges River is so wide that a person on one of its banks cannot see across to the opposite bank. After the Kosi River joins the Ganges, the river is even wider. At this point, the course of the river shifts year by year. The river erodes huge chunks of its riverbanks, and it then drops these chunks further along its course, forming new land. While one farmer might lose land, another gains more.

HOW THE GANGES PLAIN WAS FORMED

Millions of years ago, the Ganges plain was a deep valley between the Himalaya Mountains and the rest of present-day India. Rivers picked up **sediment** as they ran down the mountains. When the rivers reached the valley, they dumped their sediment. Over millions of years, the valley filled with this sediment and became a wide, flat plain.

The Lower Ganges

For thousands of years, the waters of the Ganges River joined the Hooghly River and flowed into the sea at the **mouth** of the Hooghly in northern India. In the twelfth century, however, forces beneath Earth's crust pushed the land upward, creating a slope down to present-day Bangladesh. The Ganges River now runs down this slope, flowing through Bangladesh before reaching the sea.

After the Ganges River enters Bangladesh, its official name becomes the Padma River, although this stage of the river is still called the Ganges by many people. It is then joined by the mighty Brahmaputra River, the largest tributary of the Ganges. The Meghna River enters the Ganges before it empties into the Bay of Bengal.

The Ganges Delta

The Ganges rushes into the sea with such force that a brown stain spreads out into the Bay of Bengal for 300 miles (500 km). This stain is the sediment that the Ganges and Brahmaputra Rivers have brought down from the Himalaya Mountains. Together, these rivers carry 1.97 billion tons (1.79 billion metric tons) of sediment each year. Most of this sediment is dropped in the delta before the waters of the Ganges enter the sea. The sediment forms small islands, which force the river to spread out into many shallow channels. As a result, the Ganges delta is constantly expanding.

GANGES DELTA FACTS

- The fan-shaped region between the Padma (Ganges) and Hooghly Rivers forms the delta of the Ganges. In this area, many small rivers flow into the sea.
- The Padma River in Bangladesh, the main mouth of the Ganges, is 20 miles (30 km) wide.
- The Hooghly River, in India, is considered the Gange River's second mouth. Some of the river's water reaches the sea at this mouth.
- The Ganges delta covers an area of 50,200 square miles (130,000 sq km) — about the same size as North Carolina.

In Bangladesh, not far from the Bay of Bengal, the waters
of the Ganges River have almost reached the end of their journey.

BUDDHISM

Buddhism was founded about 500 B.C. by Siddhartha Gautama, a prince who lived in the present-day Indian state of Bihar. Siddhartha later became known as Buddha, which means "the enlightened one." There are approximately 7 million Buddhists in India, as well as millions more throughout the world.

Early Settlers

About 1200 B.C., groups of people known as Aryans, from central Asia, began to arrive in the Ganges plain. The Aryans settled in the Ganges plain, where they practiced farming. With its flat land, fertile soil, and plentiful water, the river plain was ideal for farming, and the region's widespread forests provided the settlers with wood for fuel and for building houses and boats.

The Aryans spread eastward, establishing settlements along the Ganges River. Trade began between the settlements. Then, Aryan merchants began traveling down the Ganges to India's east coast, were they met traders on ships from Southeast Asia. The Aryans also began to do business on India's west coast, with merchants from Africa and the Middle East. Aryan traders reached the west coast by sailing down the Narmada River, southwest of the Ganges.

This stone statue of Siddhartha Gautama, the founder of Buddhism, was carved between A.D. 600 and 800.

HINDUISM

Hinduism was born on the Ganges plain about 1500 B.C., but its roots go back even further, to the religious practices performed by the Aryans before they came to India. Hinduism is one of the world's oldest religions. It is the largest religion in India and in Asia as a whole. In India, Hinduism has 850 million followers.

Aryan Kingdoms

The Aryan settlements gradually grew into kingdoms, the most important of which was Magadha, in the present-day Indian state of Bihar. Magadha became rich and powerful because it was able to control trade and communications up and down the Ganges River. By 500 B.C., the kingdom of Magadha ruled northern India. The kingdom's capital was Pataliputra, the site of present-day Patna.

In 303 B.C., the King of Syria sent an ambassador to Pataliputra. The ambassador described the city as being 10 miles (16 km) long and 2 miles (3 km) wide. Built on the banks of the Ganges, the city was protected by a deep moat and a high wooden fence. The city had 450,000 inhabitants living in wooden houses.

This bronze statue of Siva was made between 1200 and 1300. It depicts the Hindu god as the Lord of the Dance, trampling on a figure that is supposed to represent ignorance.

Mauryans and Guptas

About 320 B.C., a ruler named Chandragupta Maurya took control of the northern kingdom of Magadha. He built up a large empire with Pataliputra as its center. This Mauryan Empire eventually stretched north into present-day Afghanistan. Later, Chandragupta's grandson, the emperor Asoka, conquered southern India as well.

After Asoka's death, the Mauryan Empire broke up, but fame and glory returned to the kingdom of Magadha when a new **dynasty** of emperors made Pataliputra their capital. The Gupta emperors ruled between the fourth and sixth centuries A.D. During this period, there were no wars with neighboring kingdoms, and people were free to be Buddhists or Hindus. The Gupta emperors encouraged artists, musicians, and dancers.

After the Guptas, the kingdom of Magadha went into a decline and the city of Pataliputra crumbled into ruins. In the following centuries, other kingdoms along the Ganges River also faded away, weakened by attacking armies from present-day Iran and Afghanistan.

ASOKA'S PILLARS

The Mauryan emperor Asoka was a just ruler respected by his people. Asoka erected pillars throughout his empire. The pillars contained carved edicts instructing people to respect each other and nature. On top of one of the pillars were four stone lions sitting in a circle. The four lions are now the national emblem of India.

The Mogul Empire

In the 1500s, a Muslim people called Moguls eventually conquered northern India, ruling it from Delhi. The Mogul Empire lasted for over 300 years. For most of this period, the Ganges River continued to play an important role in trade and transportation. Wheat and rice grown on the banks of the Ganges, for example, were greatly in demand to feed the rapidly growing populations of Delhi and Agra.

The Mogul Empire finally came to an end in the 1850s. By then, the once great empire had split into kingdoms whose rulers were more involved in fighting each other than in keeping out foreigners.

This painting shows the Mogul emperor Shah Jahan being weighed on his birthday. Shah Jahan, who ruled from 1627 to 1658, built the famous Taj Mahal.

The British in India

As the Moguls' hold over northern India weakened, another group of foreigners began to replace them. For almost a hundred years, the British were the most powerful people in India.

British merchants from the East India Company of London began arriving on the Hooghly River in 1651. The company used its own army to conquer Bengal, a region encompassing what is now Bangladesh and the Indian state of West Bengal. Not content with this huge territory, the East India Company extended its power. By the early 1800s, the company controlled India.

The company's treatment of the Indians created discontent. In 1857, Indian soldiers, or sepoys, employed by the company rebelled. The British call this rebellion the Sepoy Mutiny, but in India it is known as the First

> **❝ *I was to hear many times: 'Before the English came, we were not poor. They took our riches, the wealth from our people. They squeezed them like juice from a lemon.'* ❞**
> Dennison Berwick,
> *A Walk along the Ganges*
> (1986)

In this photograph, Mahatma Gandhi (right) is talking to Jawaharlal Nehru, the first prime minister of India after it gained independence.

The Victoria Memorial in Kolkata (Calcutta) was built by the British while they ruled India.

War of Independence. The British quickly put down the rebellion, but many British and Indian people were killed. The British government then took control of India, and it became part of the British Empire.

Indian Independence

Although defeated in 1857, the Indian rebels did not fail completely, because their rebellion led many Indians to support Indian independence. In 1885, the first political party in India, the Indian National Congress (INC), was established. Its main objective was the creation of an independent India, free from British rule. The INC eventually had many followers, and it supported Mahatma Gandhi in 1920 when he began his peaceful opposition to British rule. Gandhi argued that words, not guns, would defeat the British, and he was proven right. The British finally left India in 1947.

As the British became less important, so did the Ganges River. By the late 1800s, the Upper Ganges Canal had made the river too shallow for large ships, and roads and railroads had been built to carry people and goods. The river was never a vital means of transportation again. The only exception is the Ganges delta, where river boats are still used today.

Chapter 3

CITIES ALONG THE GANGES

CITIES ALONG THE GANGES

Hindu pilgrims bathe at the sangam *at Allahabad during a holy festival.*

Kanpur (India)

Kanpur is the first city on the Ganges River's route to the sea. Two hundred years ago, it was a sleepy village called Cawnpore. Then the East India Company opened a **trading post** at Cawnpore and provided soldiers to protect it. The trading post boomed, and a large cantonment (military base) grew up around it. Kanpur is now the biggest city in the Indian state of Uttar Pradesh and one of the biggest and busiest cities in India. A nearby bridge over the Ganges River brings people to the city from several directions.

> 66 *Allahabad: Eight million Hindu pilgrims are expected to bathe in the Ganges River on Sunday as the massive Kumbh Mela festival reaches a climax. The festival is expected to draw 70 million people — perhaps the largest single gathering of humans ever.* 99
> CNN/Reuters News Service, January 14, 2001

Allahabad

The next city along the river after Kanpur is Allahabad, one of the oldest cities in India. A settlement has existed there since the time of the Aryan people. Today, Allahabad is one of the most sacred places for Hindus. **Pilgrims** come to bathe at the *sangam*, or meeting point, of three rivers — the Ganges, the Yamuna, and the imaginary Saraswati. According to Hindu mythology, the Saraswati surfaces at the *sangam* after flowing underground from the Himalaya Mountains. During a religious festival called Kumbh Mela, millions of Hindus line up to bathe at the *sangam*.

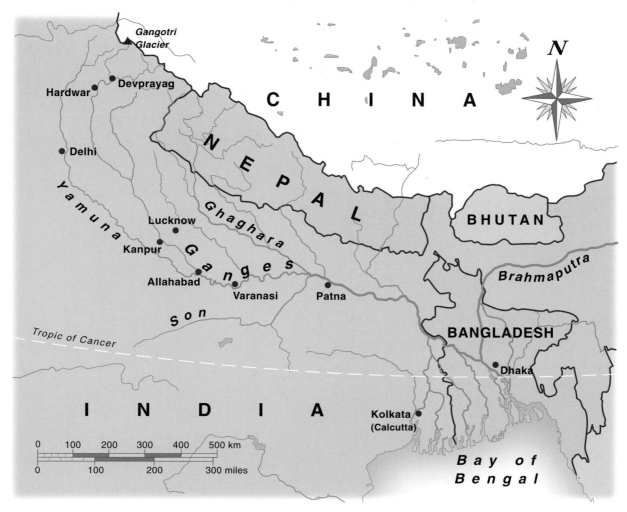

This map shows the main cities
and towns along the Ganges River.

During the Sepoy Mutiny (First War of Independence), Allahabad was the scene of fighting, and the city was one of the centers of the independence movement in India.

Allahabad was once the home of the Nehru family. Jawaharlal Nehru became the first prime minister of India after it gained its independence from the British. His daughter, Indira Gandhi, and her son, Rajiv, were also Indian prime ministers. The family's former home is now a museum.

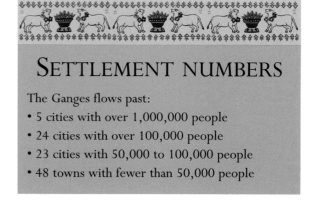

SETTLEMENT NUMBERS

The Ganges flows past:
• 5 cities with over 1,000,000 people
• 24 cities with over 100,000 people
• 23 cities with 50,000 to 100,000 people
• 48 towns with fewer than 50,000 people

Varanasi (India)

The ancient holy city of Varanasi has existed since at least the seventh century B.C. It is famous for its *ghats*, or steps, that lead down to the Ganges River. Thousands of Hindu pilgrims use these steps each year to bathe in the Ganges. After they have bathed, the pilgrims pray in some of the city's 1,500 sacred buildings.

Varanasi is an important center of learning. The city's university specializes in the study of Sanskrit, the ancient language of India, and scholars from all over India come to the city to study the language. Musicians also come to the city to learn to sing and play traditional instruments. Teachers instruct their pupils how to play the *sitar* (a guitarlike instrument) and the *tabla* (small drums). Varanasi also has many gyms where strongmen learn to perform amazing feats of strength. During the time of the British Empire, the city was known as Benares.

Patna (India)

Patna is the capital city of Bihar, which is the poorest, most crowded, and most corrupt state in India. The city is built upon the ruins of Pataliputra, a beautiful, ancient city that once attracted visitors from as far away as Europe and China. Today, however, Patna is noisy, polluted, and unsafe. The city's crime rate is very high, and gang killings are common.

> 66 *No one has ever called Patna a beautiful city; but revisiting it I found I had forgotten how bad things were. Around the garbage heaps, goats, pigs, dogs, and children compete for scraps of food. The further you go, the worse it becomes.* 99
>
> William Dalrymple, *The Age of Kali: Indian Travels and Encounters* (1998)

Hindu pilgrims use one of Varanasi's many ghats to reach the Ganges River.

> ❝ Benares [Varanasi] has for several hundred years been famous for its strongmen and its akharas (gyms). The most renowned of these is three hundred years old…and it has produced, among many others, the amazing Nanka Maharj who broke five coconuts with one blow of the fist and who fought the fearsome Ghulam Pahalwan for eleven days without yielding. ❞

Mukul Kesavan, *A Journey Down the Ganga* (1989)

Kolkata (India)

Kolkata (Calcutta) is located on the Hooghly River at the edge of the Ganges delta. It was a small fishing village until the East India Company built its second trading post there in 1686. (The company's first trading post, further upriver, had been a disaster.)

On the streets of Kolkata, cows are a common sight.

Kolkata was the capital of British India until 1911. The British called it Calcutta, and the city did not change its name back to Kolkata until 1999. Today, Kolkata is the capital of the state of West Bengal. It is the largest and most populated city in India after Mumbai (formerly called Bombay).

Many visitors to Kolkata see it as a city in crisis. They believe the city will eventually grind to a halt and collapse into chaos. These visitors point out the overcrowded slums, traffic-filled streets, and unrepaired buildings. Many people live on the streets of Kolkata, sleeping on sidewalks or in parks. Rats eat piles of uncollected garbage, and the streets are jammed with vehicles pouring out fumes.

Kolkata's inhabitants will admit there is a lot wrong with their city, but they claim that Kolkata is improving — at a very slow pace.

> **❝ Dreadful, gruesome, frightening. The world's largest slum. A disastrously overcrowded place where tens of thousands sleep in the streets, a hell of degradation and squalor, the cesspool of the world. A dying city. A vision of the end of man… ❞**
> Peter T. White, writing about Kolkata in *National Geographic* magazine, 1973

Dhaka (Bangladesh)

The city of Dhaka became important in the 1600s when the Moguls made it the capital of Bengal. It is now the capital of Bangladesh, a country formed in 1971 from what used to be East Pakistan.

Dhaka is located on the Dhaleswari River, just north of the Ganges River. The city is built on low, flat land, so it floods easily. High **embankments** have been built to protect it. After heavy rains, however, the river bursts through these barriers and floods the city's streets.

The "old city" is in the greatest danger from flooding because it is right next to the river. This ancient area of Dhaka is tightly packed with houses and small market squares connected by narrow streets. The area looks very different from Ramna Maidan, the modern, well-planned area further north. Government offices, foreign embassies, and a university have all been built in Ramna Maidan.

Buildings on the river in the "old city" of Dhaka are built on stilts to prevent them from being flooded.

Chapter 4

FARMING, TRADE, AND INDUSTRY

A riverboat carries jute to a factory in Bangladesh, where it will be made into sacks, ropes, and backing for carpets.

Farming

Farming is the main activity along the Ganges River. Cotton, **jute**, cereals, rice, **pulses**, sugar cane, fruit, and vegetables are all grown beside the banks of the river.

Although the Ganges plain and delta have fertile soil that is ideal for growing crops, heavy rains and a long, dry season between the rains can cause problems. Northern India gets most of its rain from the **monsoon**, a wind that blows in from the Indian Ocean from June to October. During these months, heavy rainstorms often cause flooding. Very little rain falls, however, during the rest of the year. Crops cannot grow when weather conditions are extremely dry, resulting in food shortages. The shortages used to be common in areas around the Ganges River during the dry season, and sometimes there was so little food that areas suffered from **famines**. The state of Bihar experienced especially severe famines. The food shortages persisted well into the twentieth century.

THE UPPER GANGES CANAL

• Took twelve years to complete
• The largest **irrigation** system in the world when it opened in 1854
• Supplies 500 miles (800 km) of irrigation channels with water

New Solutions, New Problems

As late as the 1950s and 1960s, food shortages were common on the Ganges plain. Then, in the 1970s, farmers began planting new kinds of rice and wheat seeds that produced much larger harvests. Today, shortages are rare. These new crops, however, have created new problems. They require large amounts of chemical **fertilizers** and **pesticides** to grow well, and many of these chemicals end up in the Ganges, increasing the harmful pollution in the river. The seeds and chemicals are also expensive. Many farmers borrow money to buy them and end up with large debts.

The Upper Ganges Canal has brought water to large areas of farmland in the Ganges plain. Together with the Lower Ganges Canal, it provides irrigation for 1,500,000 acres (607,000 hectares) of farmland in the Doab, an area between the Ganges and Yamuna Rivers. A regular supply of water to the Doab has allowed farmers to grow crops throughout the year and to grow enough crops to feed the huge cities of New Delhi, Agra, Kanpur, and Allahabad.

Workers put rice into sacks after it has been dried in the sun. Water from the Ganges River is used to irrigate the fields where this rice is grown.

Trade and Industry

Today, many people living near the Ganges River find it hard to earn a living from farming. They often give up and head for the cities to look for jobs in stores and factories.

Kanpur is the most industrialized city on the Ganges River. The city is home to the main manufacturers in India of leather goods such as wallets, shoes, handbags, and jackets. Kanpur also has factories that make military aircraft and guns, process food, and produce fertilizers.

Allahabad and Patna are important trading centers for crops grown on nearby farms. The crops are stored in warehouses before being sold at auctions and taken away by trains and trucks.

Silk weaving is big business in Varanasi, but unfortunately many factories employ children to keep costs down. These children work for long hours in bad conditions and are paid very little. Although there are laws banning child workers, most factory owners ignore them. The children have to work because their parents are so poor, and their families need the extra income to survive.

This boy is weaving silk on a hand loom in Varanasi. He is one of thousands employed in the silk industry in India.

In a tannery in Kanpur, animal skins are turned into leather.

KANPUR'S COTTON MILLS

During the U.S. Civil War (1861–1865), cotton from the United States did not reach Europe, so Europeans bought more cotton from India. India quickly built new cotton mills. Between 1869 and 1882, Kanpur became a "cotton city," full of huge mills. Most of the mills, however, shut down in the late twentieth century.

Silk from Varanasi is used to make beautiful **saris** embroidered with real gold thread. The saris are extremely expensive, but every Indian girl dreams of wearing one on her wedding day.

Jute is grown around the Ganges delta. It is then taken to factories in Kolkata and Dhaka, where its fibers are turned into sacks, ropes, and the backing for carpets. Cheaper artificial materials, such as plastic and nylon, have been replacing jute in recent years. As a result, some factories in these cities have been forced to close.

Transportation on the River

For hundreds of years, the Ganges River was a busy shipping route. At the time of the Mauryan and Gupta Empires, huge sailing ships carried cotton, metals, and grain along the river. Kingdoms by the river received money by charging taxes to ships passing through their territories. Many pirate ships could be found on the wider stretches of the river, where vessels could be robbed out of sight of land.

Bangladesh's waterways are always busy with boats, large and small.

The sailing ships had the river to themselves until the 1800s. In 1828, the East India Company sent a paddle wheeler upriver to see how far it could go, and it traveled as far as Allahabad. The trip took twenty-three days. By sailing ship, the same trip would have taken three months. The company ordered a fleet of paddle wheelers. In 1834, it began regular service between Kolkata and Allahabad, with stops at thirty trading stations along the way.

Changes on the River

When the Upper Ganges Canal opened in 1854, transportation on the Ganges River changed drastically. The canal drained so much water out of the river that paddle wheelers could not travel far. Large ships could reach Patna, but only smaller "country boats," with oars and sails, could travel any further. To make matters worse, the Ganges River had new rivals in the business of transportation — roads and railways.

> **The paddle steamers [wheelers] were principally used for freight as passenger fares were expensive. They were much safer from pirates, and the East India Company shipped money to pay wages, government forms, cotton seeds, and books to its stations up-country. Opium, cakes of indigo dye, silk, and shellac [to make polish and varnish] were the principal commodities carried to Calcutta [Kolkata].**
>
> Dennison Berwick, *A Walk along the Ganges* (1986)

Today, only the delta region of the Ganges River is used for transportation. In Bangladesh, the roads are bad and very few bridges exist, so travel by vehicle or train is very slow. The easiest way to get around is by boat — whether it is a canoe or a passenger ferry. Oceangoing ships can travel up the Padma River to Dhaka's port, Narayanganj. The ships can also use the Hooghly River to reach Kolkata. This trip, however, is getting more difficult for the large ships because the river has been filling up with sediment.

Chapter 5

ANIMALS AND PLANTS

Upper Ganges

Very few animals and plants can survive in the icy mountain peaks at the source of the Ganges, where temperatures are below freezing for most of the year and the ground is covered by deep snow. Further down the mountains, thick forests of pine, fir, and deodar (cedar) trees can be found. The deodars are highly prized because their tough timber is ideal for building houses, so many of the trees have been chopped down.

Sheep and goats graze on the hillsides where the trees have been cut down. These animals provide milk, as well as wool for spinning into warm clothes. Goats are also used to carry heavy loads along the narrow, steep paths between villages.

A Himalayan black bear searches for food.

PERFORMING BEARS

Trained Himalayan bears can be found all over India. The bears are captured in the wild and sold to circuses, where they learn to perform tricks. Bears are also sold to wandering musicians, who train them to "dance" for money from passersby. Circus owners and musicians usually treat a trained bear cruelly, controlling it with a leash attached to a ring through its nose. Few of these bears survive to an old age.

The remaining forests are home to Himalayan black and brown bears. Like many bears in the wild, they have been known to attack people. Trained Himalayan bears, however, are common in India. These "performing" bears are often treated badly.

The mahseer, a large fish similar to a salmon, swims in the fast-flowing waters of the upper Ganges. People come from all over the world to fish for the mahseer. It is hard to catch — but wonderful to eat!

A shepherd herds his flock of sheep and goats in the foothills of the Himalayas.

Middle Ganges

When the Aryan people first arrived on the Ganges plain, the region and the mountains beyond it were covered by forests. Since then, most of the forests have been chopped down to make way for farms, cities, roads, and railways. The forests provided shelter for animals, and, with the trees cut down, people could easily hunt them. As a result, the populations of many species have decreased dramatically. During Aryan times, for example, forests in the region were full of lions, but now only about 200 remain. The lions live in the Gir

forest, located in the state of Gujarat in northwest India. The Gir forest is one of the last areas of forest in northern India. The lions live in a conservation area, where they have protection from hunters.

The presence of humans in the Ganges plain has also had a damaging impact on animals that live in the river. The population of the Ganges River dolphin, for example, has plummeted. In the early 1980s, 4,000 to 5,000 river dolphins were believed to be living in the Ganges. The latest estimate puts their number at less than 2,000. The Ganges River dolphin is officially classified as an endangered species.

These lions live in safety in the Gir forest. Although common thousands of years ago, the animals are now in danger of dying out.

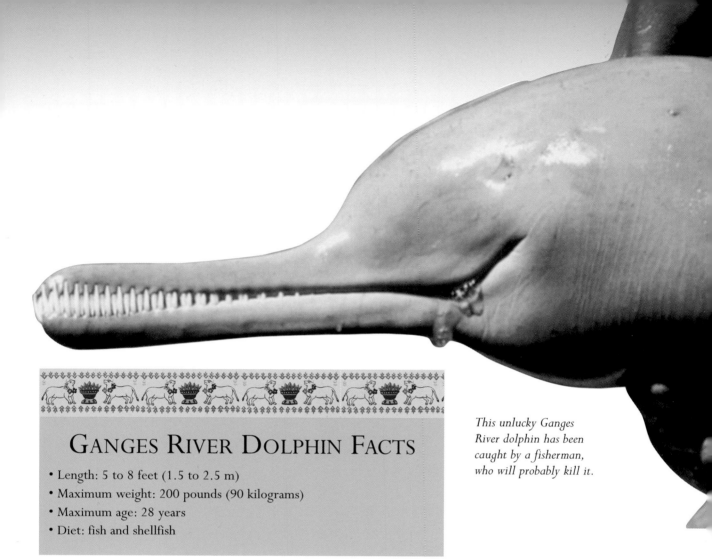

This unlucky Ganges River dolphin has been caught by a fisherman, who will probably kill it.

GANGES RIVER DOLPHIN FACTS

- Length: 5 to 8 feet (1.5 to 2.5 m)
- Maximum weight: 200 pounds (90 kilograms)
- Maximum age: 28 years
- Diet: fish and shellfish

A freshwater dolphin, the Ganges River dolphin is virtually blind, so it guides itself by swimming on one side and trailing a flipper along the muddy river bed. Ganges River dolphins are killed deliberately for their oil and blubber (a kind of fat), but they often die accidentally, when they get trapped in fishing nets. High levels of pollution in the Ganges River have also harmed the dolphins.

Some members of the animal kingdom have benefited from the human presence in the Ganges plain. Scavenger birds such as kites, crows, and vultures, for example, are common in the skies above the Ganges. They thrive on dead and rotting flesh, be it animal or human. The lammergeier (bearded vulture) is easy to spot, because it has a wingspan of over 8 feet (2.5 m). It is also looks very unappealing, with a bare head and a bent, scraggy neck.

Spiky pneumatophores poke through the mud of the Sundarbans in Bangladesh.

Lower Ganges

Most of the western delta of the Ganges is covered by thick forest. Called the Sundarbans, this forest is named after the sundari trees that flourish in the marshy land. The forest covers about 7,900 square miles (20,450 square km), an area that is more than twice the size of Delaware.

The world's largest mangrove forest is on the seaward edge of the Sundarbans and is covered by seawater at high tide. The mangrove trees have long roots known as **pneumatophores**. These roots grow up through the mud to get the trees' supply of oxygen when the tide is out. The mud contains no oxygen, so the mangrove trees would die without these roots.

Creatures of the Sundarbans

The Sundarbans has three different kinds of **habitat** — land, seawater, and freshwater. Because the forest has such a range of habitats, it contains an unusually wide variety of animals. Many creatures in the Sundarbans have adapted to life in a place that alternates between being wet and dry. The Royal Bengal tiger, for example, swims between islands in search of its prey. This tiger eats deer, wild pigs, and sometimes even humans. The Royal Bengal tiger also eats fish — a food that most tigers avoid. The mudskipper is another creature in the Sundarbans that behaves in an unusual way. This fish can actually survive out of water. At low tide, the mudskipper can be spotted hopping around on the mud — and even climbing trees!

The Sundarbans has lost many of its trees, especially in Bangladesh. This poor country has an enormous population, and its people need wood for fuel and building new homes. The Bengal tigers, in particular, have suffered as the forest has shrunk, making the animals much easier to hunt.

For hundreds of years, tigers have been killed for their skins and also their bones, which are used in China to make traditional medicines and can command a high price. The practice of hunting tigers for their skin and bones still continues today, but most tigers are now protected from hunters. The Sundarbans has been turned into a conservation area to prevent more tigers and other creatures from dying. Like the Ganges River dolphin, the Royal Bengal tiger is classified as an endangered species.

> **“** *According to the last census in 1999, there were 284 Royal Bengal tigers in the mangrove forests of the Sundarbans reserve…In 2000, 18 people, mainly fishermen, were killed by tigers in the Sundarbans.* **”**
> Reuters News Service, December 7, 2001

The last Royal Bengal tigers now live in the Sundarbans. Unlike most tigers, they are not afraid of water.

Chapter 6

ENVIRONMENTAL ISSUES

Pollution

Like many rivers in the world, the Ganges River has become increasingly polluted. Some Indians claim the Ganges is more like a foul-smelling drain than a river.

Kanpur's **tanneries** cause the greatest problems. The tanneries use poisonous chemicals to turn animal hides into leather. Before dumping the chemicals in the river, the tanneries are required by law to treat them so they are not harmful. Most tanneries, however, do not treat their chemicals.

Tannery waste flows into the Ganges River at Kanpur.

> ❝ *A well-known French physician, Dr. D. Herelle…observed some of the floating corpses [in the Ganges] of men dead of dysentery and cholera, and was surprised to find that only a few feet below the bodies, where one would expect to find millions of these dysentery and cholera germs, there were no germs at all.* ❞
>
> Sri Swami Sivananda, *Mother Ganges* (1962)

In the 1970s, farmers in the Ganges plain used large amounts of artificial fertilizers and pesticides to increase their harvests. Heavy monsoon rains washed the chemicals into the Ganges, adding even more pollution to the river.

Cities along the Ganges River grew quickly in the late twentieth century as villagers left the countryside to work in factories. The sewage systems of these cities have been unable to cope with the growing populations. As a result, much of the human waste in these cities is untreated when it is emptied into the Ganges River.

The Dutch government has been helping India clean up the Ganges River.

A Clean River?

For centuries, people have noticed that the Ganges River somehow keeps itself clean, despite its problems. The river may be dirty, but for most of its length, its water appears to be harmless to drink. Some scientists think the Ganges River contains **microorganisms** that eat germs. Experts now believe, however, that the Ganges River has become so polluted it can no longer purify itself. The Indian government is helping the river to recover. Its Ganga Action Plan, which began in 1985, has started to reduce levels of pollution in the river.

> **❝** *55 million gallons (250 million liters) of sewage is produced by Allahabad every day, but the city has the capacity to treat only 22 million gallons (100 million liters) before it spills into the river.* **❞**
>
> Interview with Anil Kumar Tiwari, lecturer in environmental science at Allahabad University, Reuters News Service, January 13, 2001

Dam Problems

In 1975, India opened the Farraka Dam. Built across the Ganges River just before the river enters Bangladesh, the dam was intended to divert water from the Ganges River into the Hooghly River. The Hooghly had been filling up with **silt**, so large ships were having difficulty reaching Kolkata. The new dam was supposed to send more water into the Hooghly River and push this silt into the sea. The dam has done its job (for now), but unfortunately it has caused other problems.

Upstream from the dam, fishermen have complained that there are fewer fish in the river. Sea fish, such as the hilsa, used to swim up the Ganges River to breed. The new dam, however, prevents the fish from swimming upstream. The fishermen fear that their catch will disappear from the river.

This new land was formed from the sediment left by the Ganges River as it enters the sea.

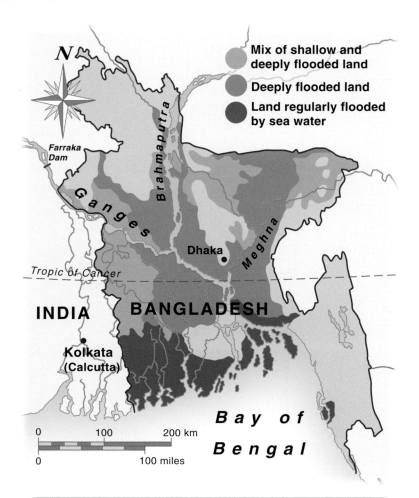

Mix of shallow and deeply flooded land

Deeply flooded land

Land regularly flooded by sea water

This map shows how Bangladesh is affected by floods in the Ganges River delta.

> **6 6** *Calcutta's [Kolkata's] port is slowly dying, due to the river silting up and the difficulty and danger encountered by big, modern ships in reaching the port.... The port's life has been extended 20 years by a barrage [Farraka Dam]...but Calcutta will eventually join the long list of silted-up ports along the Ganga.* **9 9**
> Dennison Berwick, *A Walk along the Ganges* (1986)

Water Conflicts

The Bangladeshi government also considers the Farraka Dam to be a problem. The government believes India is taking too much water from the Ganges River, especially during the dry season. The western half of the river, the government claims, is dying. Rivers in Bangladesh have less water, so seawater can travel further up the Ganges delta. Land is absorbing this salty water and becoming unfit for farming.

On December 12, 1996, the Indian and Bangladeshi governments signed a treaty to share the waters of the Ganges River. This treaty was supposed to put an end to years of squabbling, but unfortunately it has not. The question of who gets the river's water — and how much — is still a sore point between the two countries.

Floods and Cyclones

During the dry season, Bangladesh suffers from a shortage of water. During the wet season, however, too much water is a problem. In June, the monsoon brings heavy rains that rapidly fill the rivers. During this same period, more water pours into the rivers from melting snow and ice in the Himalayas. Bangladesh's rivers cannot hold all this water, so the rivers burst their banks and flood the land.

These floods are made worse by fierce storms called cyclones that form over the Bay of Bengal. The storms can create winds of 155 miles (250 km) an hour that push huge tidal waves in front of them. These huge waves can be 30 feet (9 m) tall, and they can do terrible damage to Bangladesh's coast, wiping out whole villages in minutes.

This Bangladeshi village has been badly damaged by a cyclone.

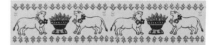

DEFORESTATION

An alarming number of trees in the Himalaya Mountains have been cut down, and this **deforestation** has contributed to flooding. The roots of trees bind the soil together, and their leaves shelter it from heavy rain. Without any trees to protect the ground, the rain washes large amounts of soil into the rivers.

On a riverbank near Dhaka, bags of sand are stacked to prevent flood damage.

These tidal waves also surge up the rivers of the Ganges delta. In 1985, seawater was forced 90 miles (145 km) inland by a cyclone. The seawater poured over the rivers' embankments and ruined the fields along them.

Causes of Floods

Although nature is usually blamed for the floods in Bangladesh, the country's inhabitants are largely responsible for the flooding. The government of Bangladesh does not have enough money to teach its people how to take care of the land. As a result, many farmers along the riverbanks allow their animals to overgraze (eat too much grass in a particular area). Most farmers also do not practice **crop rotation**, so the soil in their fields is extremely thin. When the monsoon rains come, the water runs off the fields instead of sinking into the soil.

In addition, deforestation in the Himalaya Mountains has caused large amounts of soil to be washed off the land and into the rivers. The Ganges and Brahmaputra Rivers both carry huge loads of sediment. When this sediment is deposited in the Ganges delta, the rivers in the delta become shallower. A shallower river holds less water, leading to more flooding.

SHELTERS AND EARLY WARNING

The Bangladeshi government has spent a large amount of money on cyclone shelters. It has also established an early warning system, so people will know in advance that a cyclone is coming. The results have been impressive. In 1991, a cyclone killed 139,600 people. In 1997, a cyclone warning gave 300,000 people a chance to use the shelters. Only 95 people died in the storm.

Chapter 7

BATHING AND PRAYING

BATHING AND PRAYING

Pilgrimages

All Hindus try to make a pilgrimage to the Ganges at least once in their lives. Pilgrims visit one of the many sacred places along the river, such as Hardwar, Allahabad, and Varanasi. At these sites, the pilgrims bathe in the waters of the holy river. Hindus believe the goddess Ganga washes away all their sins just as she cleans the dirt off their bodies.

Those people lucky enough to live next to the river bathe in it at least once a day. They bathe at the same time as they say their prayers, which is usually sunrise.

Clothes are laid out to dry after being washed in the Ganges River.

The pilgrims return home with some water from the Ganges because they believe the water cures the sick. They also believe the Ganges water's special power can be transferred to other water. If some Ganges water is added to a bucket of tap water, that water becomes holy and is able to make people better.

Hindus believe that if they die by the Ganges River, all their sins will be forgiven and their soul will go straight to Heaven. Most Hindus, however, die far from the river. In this case, relatives of the dead person will try to take the person's ashes to the Ganges and scatter them on the water. Hindus are always **cremated** instead of buried.

Just Another River?

Most people in Bangladesh (as well as some people in India) are Muslims who practice Islam. The Ganges River has no special role to play in the religion of Islam, and for Muslims it is just another river. For many inhabitants of Bangladesh, however,

Pilgrims carry offerings of flowers at a Hindu festival.

the Ganges is still an extremely valuable resource. Like their Indian neighbors, most Bangladeshis who live close to the Ganges River do not have running water in their homes. They wash themselves, their clothes, their pots and pans, their animals, and even their vehicles in the river. They use river water for cooking and for drinking, and they also travel more on water than on land.

Chapter 8

THE FUTURE

THE FUTURE

The Indian government has big plans for the Ganges River. It has considered connecting the Ganges to a series of canals to irrigate the dry lands of central and southern India. A canal linking the Ganges to the Brahmaputra River is also being considered, as is a dam across the Brahmaputra. The main aim of these plans is to create a steady flow of water in the Ganges River throughout the year.

The government of Bangladesh is keeping a careful eye on these proposals. It welcomes any measures that will lessen its country's floods, as well as any plans that might ensure a constant flow of water to the dying western delta. Since the construction of the Farraka Dam, however, the Bangladeshi government has mistrusted the government of India.

Even if plans for the new dam and canals are approved, their construction will take many years. Bangladesh, meanwhile, has to contend with floods right now, and people do not agree on the best way to handle the problem. The World Bank has begun an initiative called the Flood Action Plan to tame the Ganges. Since 1991, it has been strengthening, straightening, and raising riverbanks. Critics insist that the river cannot be tamed and that these measure are a waste of time. They argue that the money would be better spent on building shelters and improving a flood-warning system.

Difficult Problems

One cause of flooding — deforestation — is outside of Bangladesh's control. Many trees have been cut down in India, Nepal, and China, close to the sources of the Ganges and Brahmaputra Rivers. While China appears unconcerned about deforestation, India and Nepal support the planting of new trees on their highlands. New forest growth may help reduce the amount of soil being washed into rivers that eventually reach Bangladesh.

Global warming is another problem for the Ganges River. Glaciers in the Himalaya Mountains supply three-quarters of the water in the Ganges. As temperatures throughout the world increase, however, these glaciers are melting much faster than in the past. Experts predict that one-fifth of the glaciers in the Himalayas will have disappeared by 2035. As the glaciers melt, floods in the Ganges delta will become much worse. Once the glaciers have gone, the Ganges will have much less water, especially during the dry season.

Troubled times certainly lie ahead for the Ganges River. The good news is that governments are aware of its problems and are trying to solve them.

Poor farming practices have damaged the soil on this Himalayan hillside. When heavy rains come, more water and soil will end up in the Ganges River.

GLOSSARY

basin: the area of land drained by a river and its tributaries.

cremate: to burn a dead body so it is reduced to ashes.

crop rotation: the practice of planting different crops in the same field each year.

deforestation: the clearing of a forest.

delta: a flat, triangular area where a river empties into a large body of water, such as an ocean, through many channels.

dynasty: a succession of rulers belonging to the same family.

embankment: a high bank constructed along a river to prevent flooding.

erode: to wear away gradually.

famine: an extreme shortage of food among a large segment of a population.

fertilizer: a substance that is spread on soil to help crops grow.

glacier: a huge mass of slowly moving ice.

global warming: a process in which certain gases in the atmosphere absorb more heat, raising the temperature of Earth's climates.

gorge: a valley with extremely steep sides.

habitat: the place where a plant or animal lives and grows.

irrigation: a process of providing water to farmland through a system of channels.

jute: a plant with strong, ropelike stems.

microorganisms: creatures that cannot be seen without a microscope.

monsoon: a strong, seasonal wind that blows over the Indian Ocean and southern Asia and brings heavy rains.

mouth: the place where a river empties into a large body of water, such as an ocean.

pesticides: chemicals that are used to kill insects that damage crops but that are often harmful to wildlife and humans.

pilgrim: a person who travels to pray at a particular holy site.

pneumatophores: roots found on some plants that can take in oxygen.

pulse: a bean, pea, or lentil seed.

sari: a long piece of cloth that some Indian women wear as a dress.

sediment: pieces of dirt and rock that are deposited by rivers and glaciers.

silt: small particles of dirt and rock that are found in a river.

source: the point of origin for the waters of a river or stream.

tanneries: factories that process animal skins into leather.

trading post: a site in a lightly settled region where people exchange local goods.

tributaries: small streams or rivers that feed into larger rivers.

FURTHER INFORMATION
FURTHER INFORMATION

TIME LINE

B.C.

1200	Aryan people settle in the Ganges plain.
563	Siddhartha Gautama, or "Buddha," is born in the present-day Indian state of Bihar.
321-187	Reign of the Mauryan Empire.

A.D.

320	Reign of Gupta Empire begins.
1526	Reign of Mogul Empire begins.
1651	Agents of the East India Company arrive on the Hooghly River.
1854	Upper Ganges Canal opens.
1857	Sepoy Mutiny (First War of Independence).
1858	British government takes control of India.
1885	Indian National Congress founded.
1920	Mahatma Gandhi begins campaign against British rule.
1947	India gains independence.
1971	Bangladesh is formed.
1975	Farraka Dam opens.
1996	India and Bangladesh sign water-sharing treaty.

BOOKS

Barter, James. *The Ganges.* (Lucent Books, 2002)

Kalman, Bobbie. *India: Lands, Peoples, and Cultures* (series). (Crabtree, 2000)

Lal, Sunandini Arora. *India.* (Gareth Stevens, 1999)

Montgomery, Sy. *The Man-eating Tigers of the Sundarbans.* (Houghton Mifflin, 2001)

Whyte, Mariam. *Bangladesh.* (Marshall Cavendish, 1999)

WEB SITES

Daily Life in Ancient India
http://members.aol.com/ Donnclass/Indialife.html
Intriguing facts about ancient life in the Ganges River basin.

The Ganga Basin
www.cs.albany.edu/~amit/ ganges.html
Includes information about the Ganges River's source, tributaries, and dams.

Ganges River India
www.karlgrobl.com/Ganges/
A gallery of photographs of the Ganges River and its settlements and people.

Ganges River Dolphin
www.cetacea.org/ganges.htm
Provides facts about the size, habitat, and behavior of the Ganges River dolphin, as well as a photograph of the dolphin.

The Maha Kumbh Mela Site
www.kumbhmela.com
Information on the Kumbh Mela festival, with many photographs.

River Ganges
www.thewaterpage.com/ ganges.htm#delta
Includes information about the 1996 water-sharing treaty between India and Bangladesh.

INDEX
INDEX

Numbers in **boldface** type refer to illustrations and maps.

Alaknanda River **6**, 7, **7**
Allahabad, India 4, 8, 18, **18**, 19, **19**, 25, 26, 29, 37, 42
animals 30–35, **30, 31, 32, 33, 35**
Aryans 12, 13, 18, 32
Asoka, Emperor 14

Bay of Bengal 4, 10, 11
bears 30, **30**
Bhagirathi River **6**, 7, **7**
birds 33
boats **5**, 9, **9**, **11**, 24, **24**, 28, **28**, 29
Brahmaputra River **6**, 10, **19**, **39**, 41, 44
British, the 5, 16, 17, 19, 22
Buddhism 5, 12, 14

canals 8, 17, 24, 25, 29, 44
cyclones 40, 41

deforestation 40, 41, 44
deodar (cedar) trees 30
Devprayag, India 7, **7**, **19**
Dhaka, Bangladesh 4, **19**, 23, **23**, 27, 29, **39**
dolphins 32, 33, **33**

East India Company 16, 18, 19, 22, 29

farming 4, 9, 12, 24–25, **25**, 26, 37, 41, **45**
Farraka Dam 38, 39, **39**, 44

fish 31, 34, 38
fishing **9**, 31, 38
flooding 5, 23, 24, **39**, 40, 41, 44, 45

Gandhi, Indira 19
Gandhi, Mahatma 17, **17**
Gandhi, Rajiv 19
Ganges delta 4, 10, 17, 22, 24, 29, 39, **39**, 41, 44, 45
Ganges plain 8, 9, 12, 24, 25, 32, 33
Gangotri glacier 6, **6**, 7, **19**
Gaumukh 6, 7
global warming 45
Gupta Empire 14, 28

Hardwar, India 8, **19**, 42
Himalaya Mountains 4, 6, **6**, 9, 10, 18, **31**, 40, 41, 45, **45**
Hinduism 5, 13, 18, 20, 21, 42, 43
Hooghly River **6**, 10, 16, 22, 29, 38

Indian National Congress (INC) 17
industry 26, 27, **26, 27**
irrigation 24, 25, 44

Kanpur, India 4, 18, **19**, 25, 26, 27, **27**, 36, **36**
Kolkata (Calcutta), India 4, **17**, **19**, 22, **22**, 27, 29, 38, 39, **39**
Kumbh Mela festival 18

Lakshman Jhula 8, **8**
lions 32, **32**

Magadha, kingdom of 13, 14
Mauryan Empire 14, 28
Moguls 14, **15**, 23
monsoon 24, 40, 41
Mumbai (Bombay), India 22

Nehru, Jawaharlal **17**, 19

Padma River **6**, 10, 29
Pataliputra 13, 14, 20
Patna, India 4, 8, 9, **19**, 20, 26, 29
pilgrims **4**, 18, **18**, 20, **21**, 42, 43, **43**
pollution 5, 25, 36, **36**, 37,

Royal Bengal Tigers 34, 35, **35**

Sepoy Mutiny (First War of Independence) 16, 19
Shah Jahan 14, **15**
ships 28, 29, 39
silk 26, **26**, 27
Sundarbans 34, **34**, 35, **35**

trade 12, 18, 26, 29
transportation 17, 28, 29, **28**

Upper Ganges Canal 8, 17, 24, 25, 29

Varanasi, India 4, 5, **5**, **19**, 20, 21, **20–21**, 26, **26**, 42